VERMONT

IS WHERE YOU FIND IT

Other Books by Keith W. Jennison
available from The Countryman Press

"Yup...Nope" & Other Vermont Dialogues

The Maine Idea

Remember Maine

VERMONT

IS WHERE YOU FIND IT

Stories and pictures arranged by

KEITH WARREN JENNISON

THE COUNTRYMAN PRESS, WOODSTOCK, VERMONT

ISBN 0-88150-070-4

Printed in the United States of America by Thomson-Shore, Inc.

TO THE ROADS THAT TAKE PEOPLE HOME

Most of these stories and sayings I heard in Vermont, but that's no sign I wouldn't have heard them anywhere else in America. Many of them have appeared in print in one form or another—but beyond any book they have been kept alive in the speech and idiom of a tough-minded, high-hearted people.

K. W. J.

VERMONT

IS WHERE YOU FIND IT

1

Nice little place you have.

Lived here all your life?

Not yet, Mister.

2

How long will it take me to get to town?

How fast are you going to walk?

3

How much did you get for them pigs you sold last week, Jesse?

Not as much as I figgered I might,

but I never thought I would.

4

If we go to war, I'm coming up here to Vermont, buy a farm and forget about the world.

'Twon't do you much good, son. Very shortly after the United States goes to war Vermont'll be in it too.

5

How far is it to Fairfax?

Dunno.

Does this road go to Fairfax?

Dunno.

Say, you don't know much, do you?

Nope ... but I ain't lost.

6

Think it's going to rain, Grandma?

Be a long dry spell if it don't.

7

When I was in school they tried to teach
me that the earth goes around the sun . . .

but I knew better because I can see it coming up in the morning and going down at night.

8

Is this the Barre Road?

No, but it'll get you there.

9

How are the crops this year?

Not so good for a good year,
but not so bad for a bad year.

10

One of the best things about quiltin' is
that it gives the womenfolks something
to think about while they talk.

11

Them graves you been digging, Arnold,
they ain't wide enough, nor long enough,
nor deep enough.

Wal, you ain't heard of nobody gettin' out of them, have you?

12

What do you know today . . . for sure?

Not a damn thing.

13

Hey, you, how do I get to the Plattsburg Ferry?

If I was going to the Plattsburg Ferry
I wouldn't start from here.

14

I'd like to buy some of that breakfast food they been talking about on the radio.

We don't carry it any more.

It sells too fast.

15

One thing we've noticed about the city folks who are moving up this way...

in the old days we used to eat in the house and go to the bathroom in the yard. These new folks do it just the opposite.

16

Nice lot of sheep up there on the hill, Pop.
'Bout ready for shearin' too.

'Pears so ... from this side.

17

How'd the wheel get broke?

Hired man run her over a stone.

That the same hired man what ruin't your daughter?

Yup.

Clumsy, hain't hc.

18

If you keep them hens penned up closer they'd feed faster.

What's a hen's time worth?

19

How did you ever find the horse
everybody's been looking for, sonny?

I thought if I was a horse where would I go
and I went and he had.

20

The whole world may be going to hell,

but we ain't got time to worry
about the details.

21

The doctor thinks maybe

Uncle Pete's lost his mind...

but he don't seem to miss it none.

22

What do you do up here in the winter when the road's blocked?

We just set and think ... mostly set.

23

What do you raise around here?

Men.

24

When I think of what you have meant to me
for all these years, sometimes it's more than
I can stand not to tell you so.

25

Whereas, and heretofore nothwithstanding . . .

What's he talkin' about?

He don't say.

26

We raise more corn...

to feed more cows . . .

to get more milk . . .

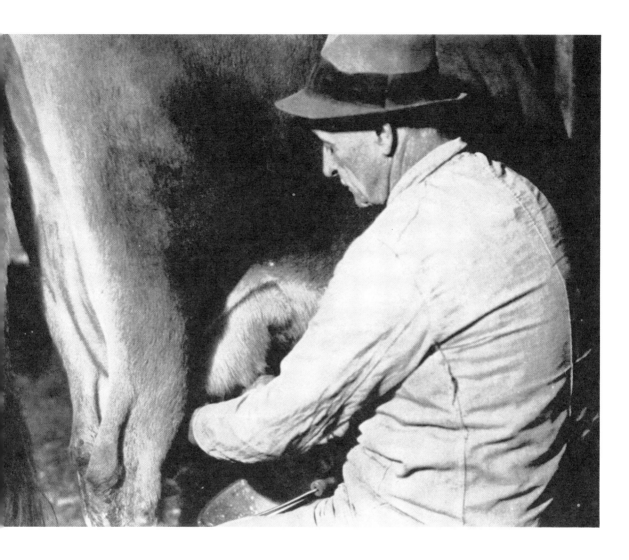

to make more money . . .

to buy more land . . .

to raise more corn . . .

INDEX AND PICTURE CREDITS

The pictures by J. W. McManigal, George French, H. W. Fechner, John Vondell, Ward Starbuck, and J. V. D. Bucher are included through the courtesy of Robert Nesmith & Associates.